For Giles – who is often awake in the moonlight.

BOXER BOOKS Ltd. and the distinctive Boxer Books logo are trademarks of Union Square & Co., LLC.

Union Square & Co., LLC, is a subsidiary of Sterling Publishing Co., Inc.

© 2025 Alexandra Milton

All rights reserved. No part of this publication may be reproduced, stored in a retrieval system, or transmitted in any form or by any means (including electronic, mechanical, photocopying, recording, or otherwise) without prior written permission from the publisher.

First published in Great Britain in 2025 by Boxer Books Limited.

ISBN HB: 978-1-4547-1286-2
ISBN PB: 978-1-4547-1287-9

A catalogue record of this book is available from the British Library.

For information about custom editions, special sales, and premium purchases, please contact specialsales@unionsquareandco.com.

Printed in China

2 4 6 8 10 9 7 5 3 1

05/25

unionsquareandco.com

Shutterstock.com (artist reference):
Edwin Godinho (wildcat); Nynke van Holten (hedgehog)

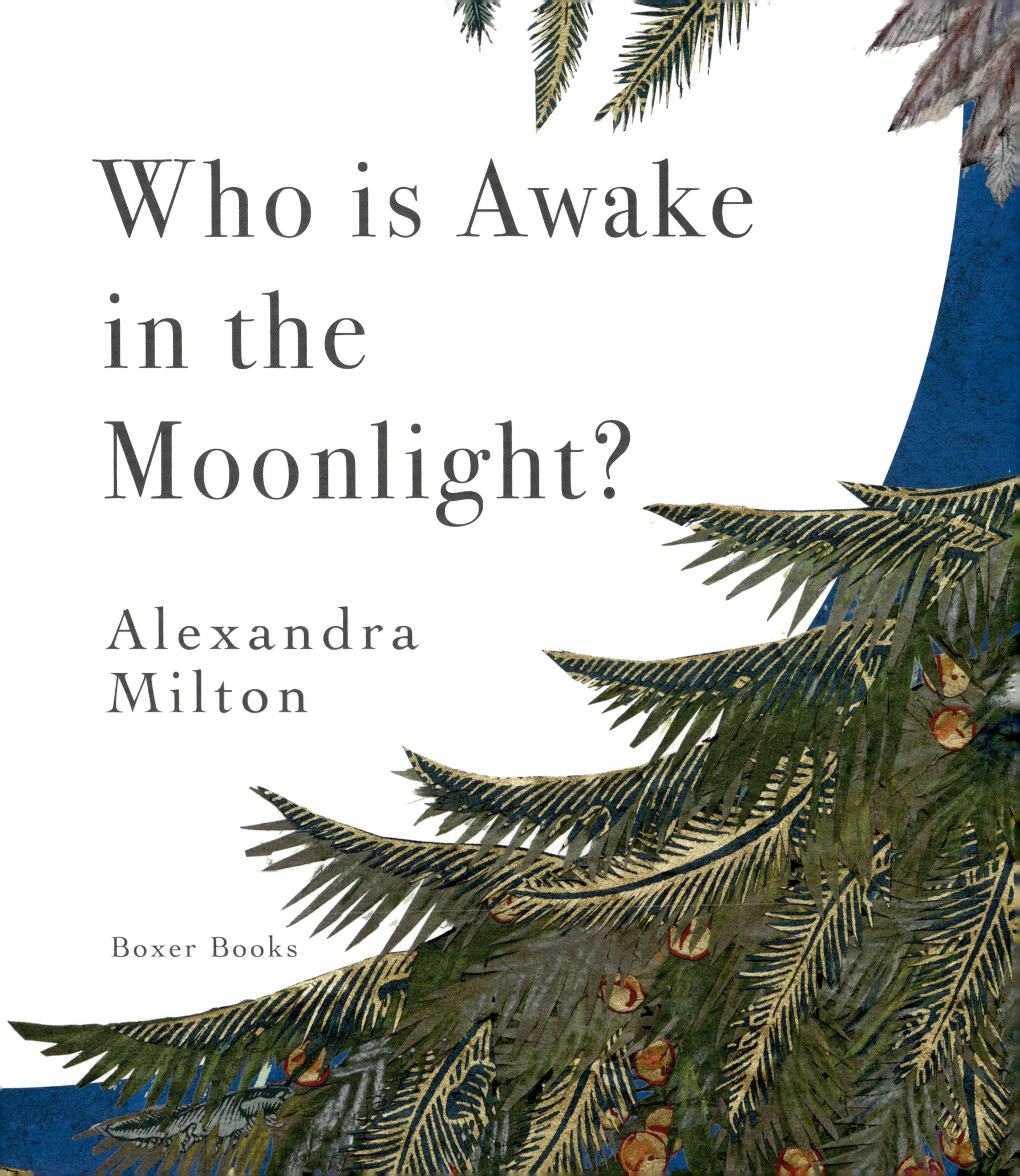

Who is Awake in the Moonlight?

Alexandra Milton

Boxer Books

All is quiet
in the sleepy old house,
Not a word, not a whisper,
not a sound to be heard.

But out in the garden,
in the light of the moon,
A rustle of leaves,
in the branches of trees.

Who is awake in the moonlight?

Dormice

Dormice sleep in the day and are awake at night. When it's dark, they can search for food without being seen. They use their long whiskers to feel their way.

The swish of a tail
and a faint miaow.

Who is awake
in the moonlight?

Cats

Cats hunt at night, because this is when the animals they like to eat are roaming around. The soft pads under cats' paws allow them to walk so quietly that their prey don't hear them coming.

A croakity-croak from the moonlit pond.

Who is awake
in the moonlight?

Frogs

Frogs avoid the heat of the sun. At night, when it is cooler, they gather together and croak to attract their mates.

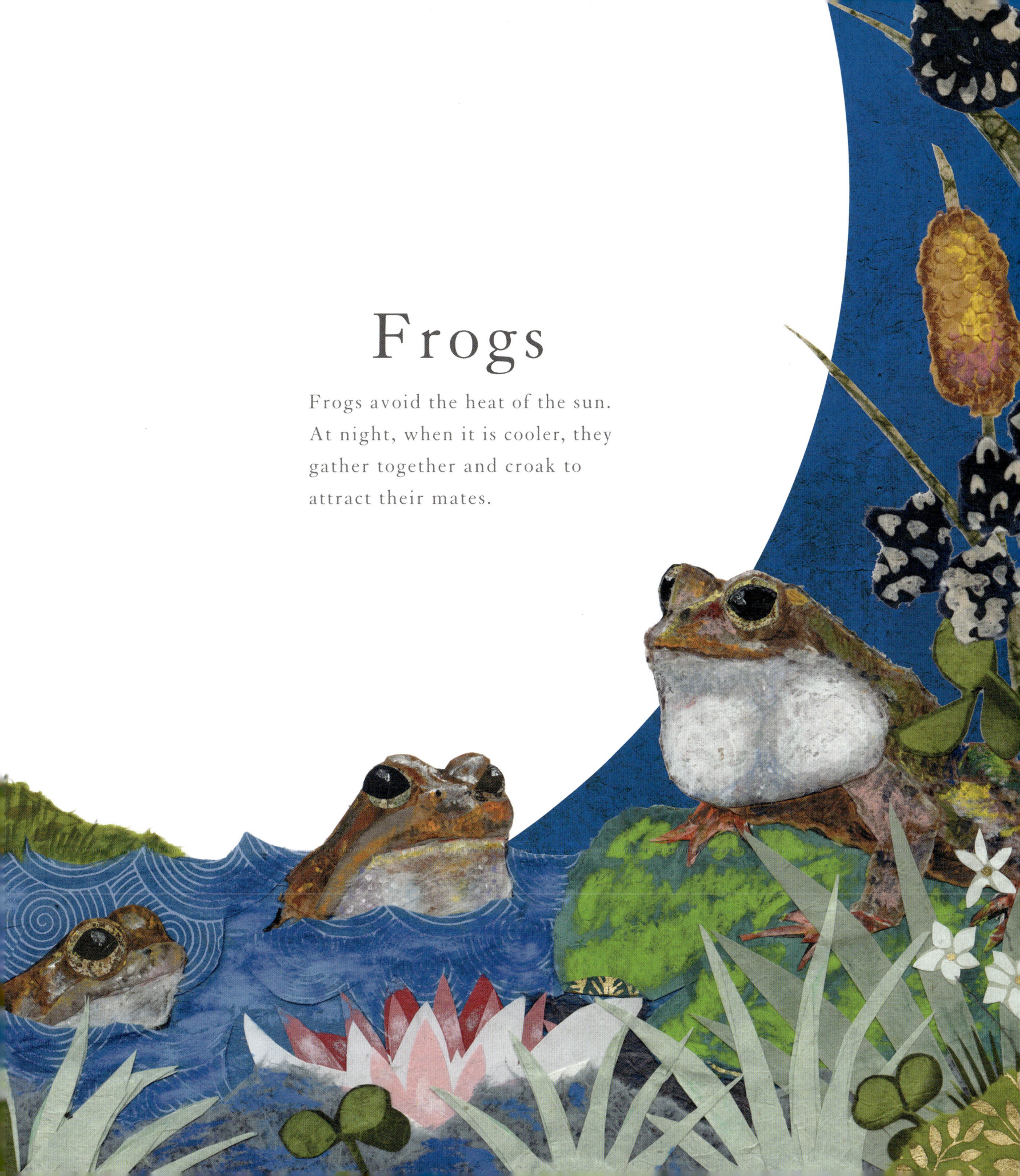

A soft low hoot and
the whooshing of wings.

Who is awake
in the moonlight?

Owls

Owls hunt at night when other birds of prey are asleep. Their extra-large eyes help them see in the dark.

A pitter and a patter
and some noisy grunts.

Who is awake
in the moonlight?

Hedgehogs

Hedgehogs are noisy eaters! To find food they use their excellent sense of smell, which can detect a worm under eight centimetres of soil. They sometimes walk up to three kilometres a night looking for food.

All is still quiet
in the sleepy old house,
But now, in the garden,
there's a faint streak of light,
And chirping and singing,
all happy and bright.

Who is awake at
the end of the night?

Songbirds

A few songbirds, such as nightingales and song thrushes, sing at night because it is quieter and the mates they hope to attract can hear them more clearly.